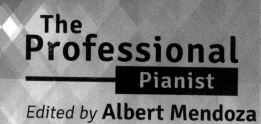

The Professional Pianist

Edited by **Albert Mendoza**

Classical

40 Piano Masterworks in Their Original Form

C000171495

This edition provides a valuable resource of accessible masterworks for busy pianists. It contains 40 piano pieces in their original form appropriate for weddings, funerals, receptions, and other events. To make the selections useful as background music, only short pieces have been included and flashy, concert-like works have been avoided. Much of the repertoire will be familiar to classical pianists, while some lesser-known gems will be delightful to discover. Each piece has been carefully engraved for easy reading, and approximate performance times have been included to assist with planning.

These masterworks are reproduced from early sources, with much effort given to preserve the composers' original intentions. To create a practical performing edition for pianists, editorial suggestions for tempos and dynamics have been added in the Baroque works (of Bach and Paradisi), where no such performance directions are found in the original sources. These may be adapted at the performer's discretion. The remaining pieces contain the composers' original tempos, dynamic markings, slurs, and articulations, with any editorial suggestions or clarifications given in parentheses. All fingering is editorial except for those set in italics, which are original fingerings by the composers. Suggested realizations for ornaments, based on period-performance practices, are given in footnotes. All pedaling and metronome marks are editorial unless otherwise noted. When multiple approximate performance times are given, the first indicates the duration of the piece without repeats taken, the second with repeats taken.

Alfred Music
P.O. Box 10003
Van Nuys, CA 91410-0003
alfred.com

ISBN-10: 1-4706-2030-8
ISBN-13: 978-1-4706-2030-1

Allemande
(from *French Suite No. 4 in E-flat Major*, BWV 815)

Johann Sebastian Bach
(1685–1750)

Gavotte

(from *French Suite No. 5 in G Major*, BWV 816)

Johann Sebastian Bach
(1685–1750)

ⓐ Play the roll *on the beat.*

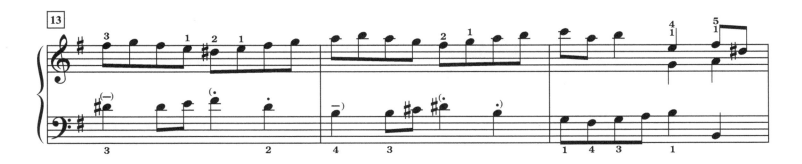

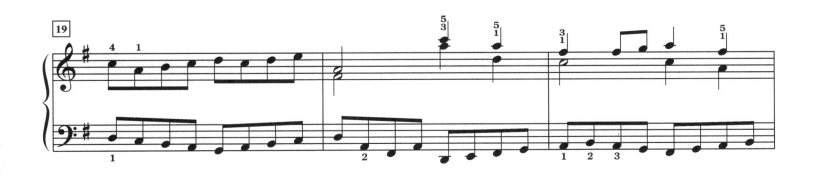

Prelude in A-flat Major
(from *The Well-Tempered Clavier, Book 1*)

Johann Sebastian Bach (1685–1750)
BWV 862

ⓐ Cadential trills in measures 17 and 34

ⓑ Inverted mordent: Play similarly in measures 38, 41, and 42.

Prelude in C Major
(from *The Well-Tempered Clavier, Book 1*)

Johann Sebastian Bach (1685–1750)
BWV 846

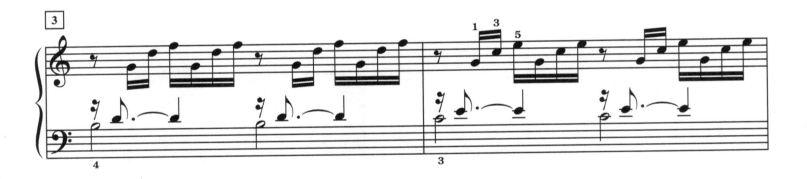

ⓐ Finger-pedal the right hand throughout: 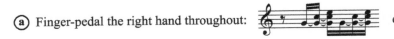 etc.

Für Elise

Ludwig van Beethoven (1770–1827)
WoO 59

ⓐ The slurs are editorial throughout.

ⓑ Beethoven included only two dynamic markings, the **pp** here and in measure 79. The other dynamics are editorial.

© Play the grace notes in measures 25 and 28 quickly, *on the beat*.

d Finger-pedal the left hand: etc.

Adagio cantabile
(from *Piano Sonata No. 8 in C Minor, "Pathétique,"* Op. 13)

Ludwig van Beethoven
(1770–1827)

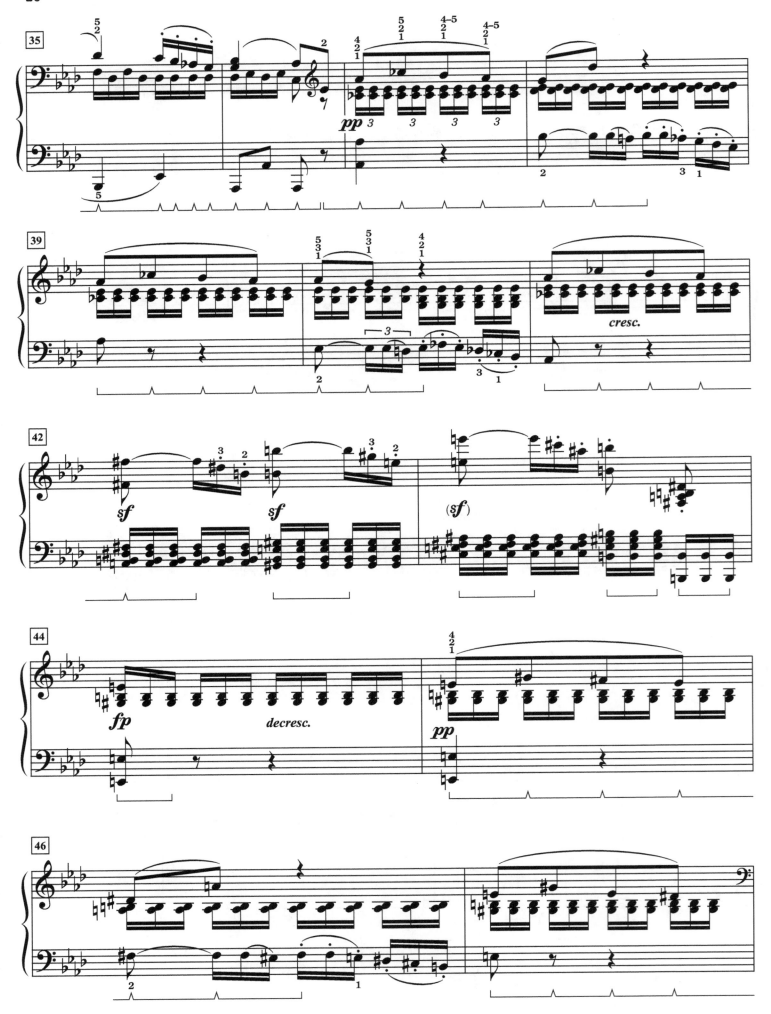

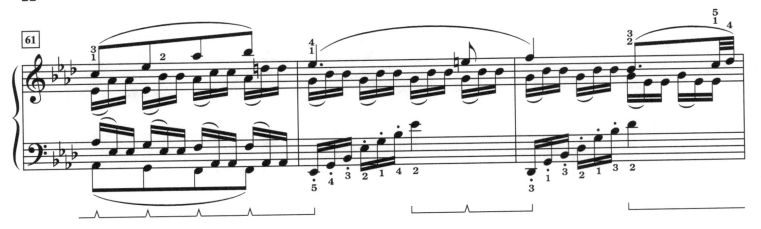

 ⓓ Play the grace notes quickly, *on the beat.*

Minuet in G Major

Ludwig van Beethoven (1770–1827)
WoO 10, No. 2

TRIO

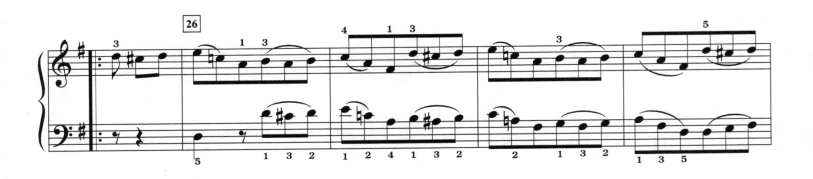

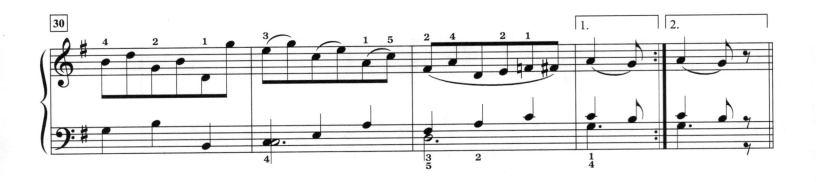

MINUET 35

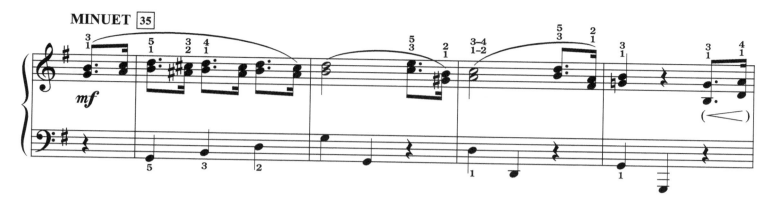

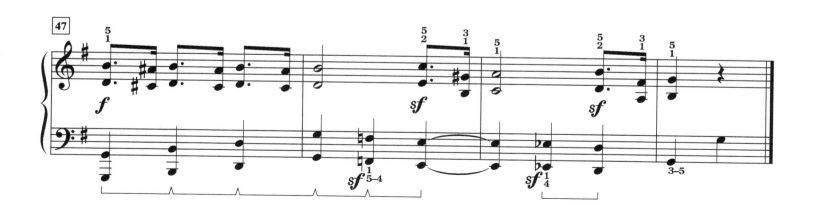

Intermezzo in E-flat Major

Johannes Brahms (1833–1897)
Op. 117, No. 1

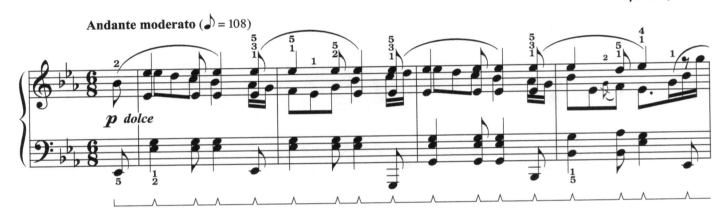

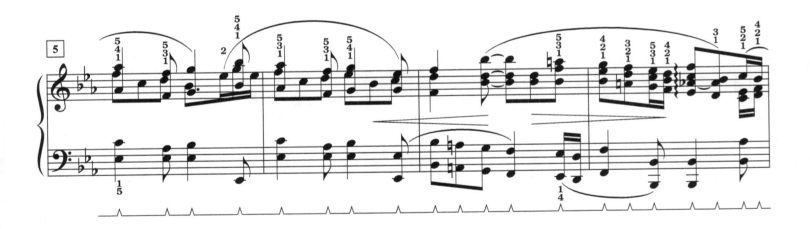

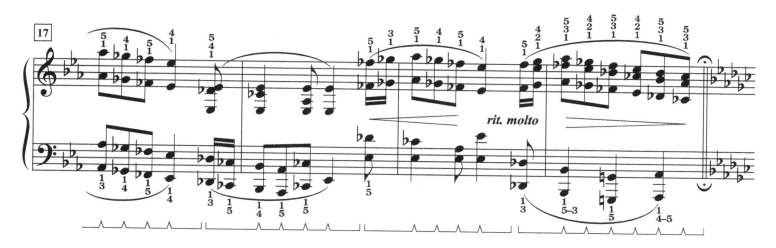

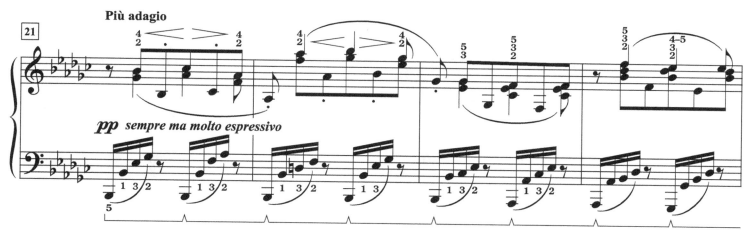

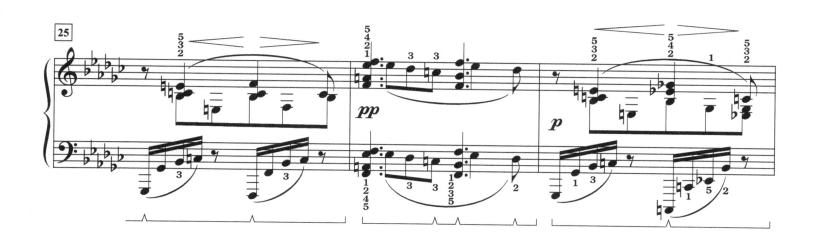

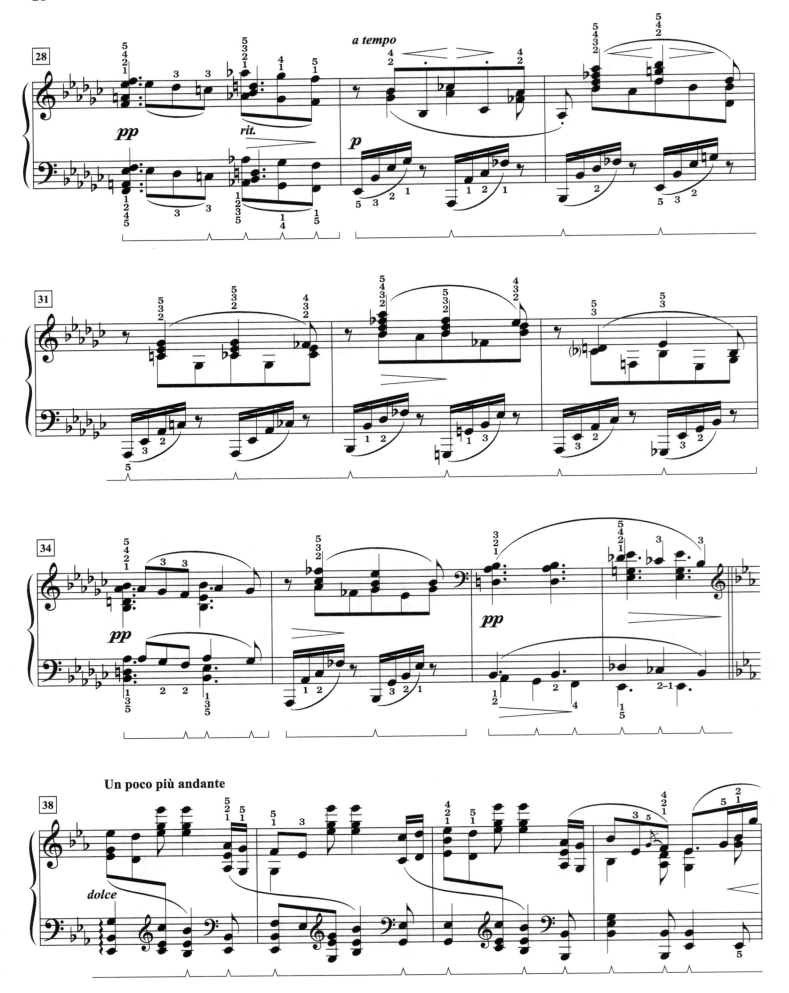

Waltz in A-flat Major

Johannes Brahms (1833–1897)
Op. 39, No. 15

ⓐ Brahms (as well as Schumann) notated the swells on one beat to suggest a vibrato-like effect, like a more intense version of a tenuto. Perform them with gentle emphasis and perhaps slight rubato.

Andante

(from *Sonatina in C Major,* Op. 36, No. 1)

Muzio Clementi
(1752–1832)

Nocturne in E-flat Major

Frédéric Chopin (1810–1849)
Op. 9, No. 2

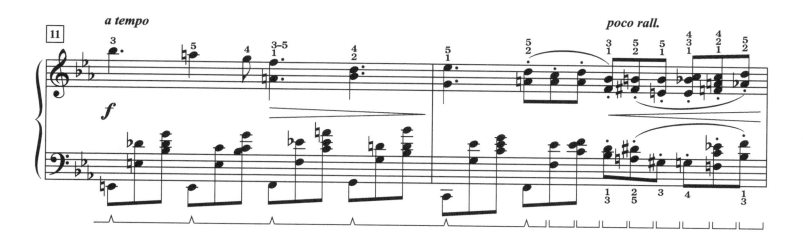

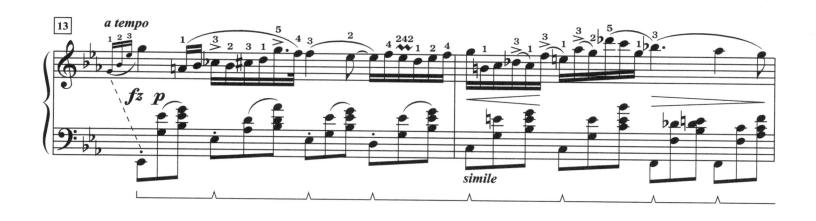

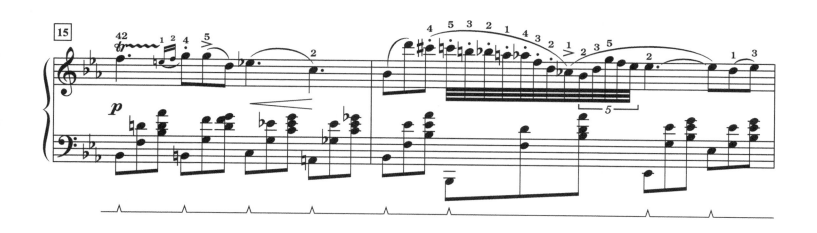

Waltz in A Minor

Frédéric Chopin (1810–1849)
Op. Posth. (B. 150)

Clair de lune

(from *Suite bergamasque*, L. 75)

Claude Debussy
(1862–1918)

(louder and livelier little by little)
peu à peu cresc. et animé

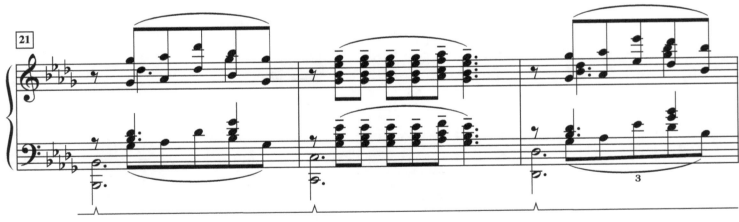

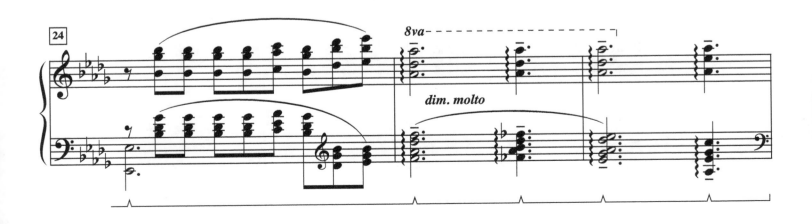

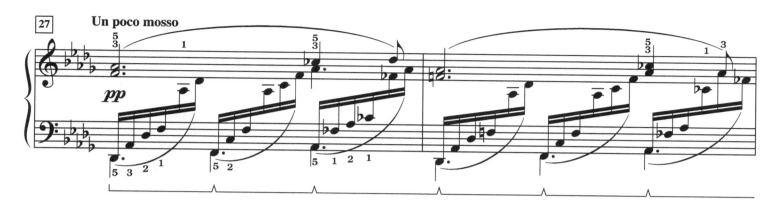

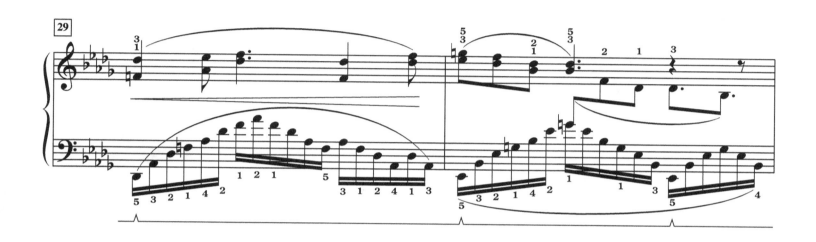

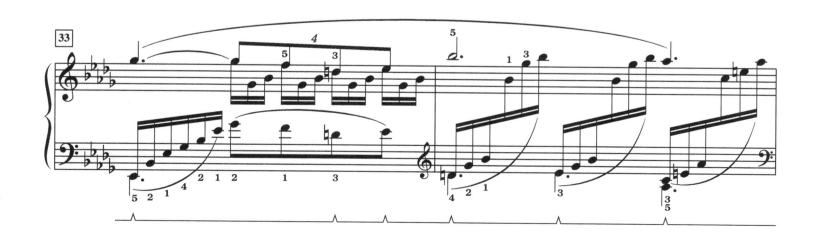

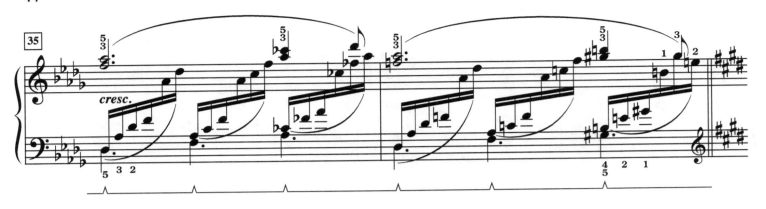

(Becoming more lively)
En animant

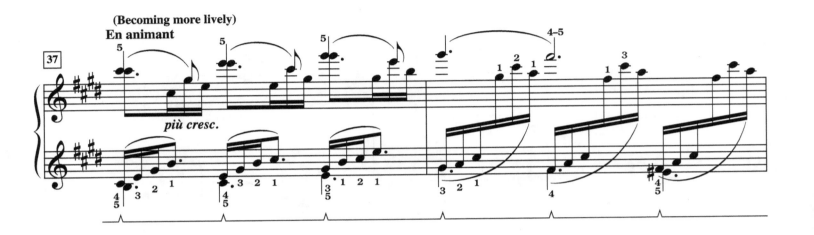

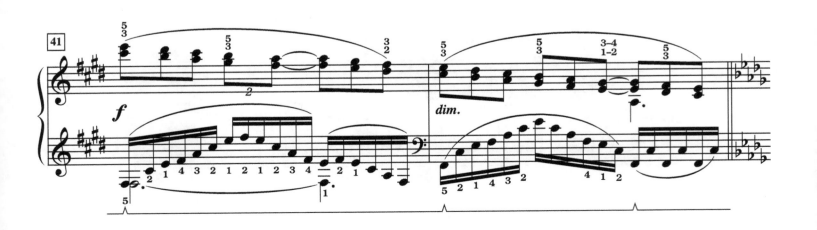

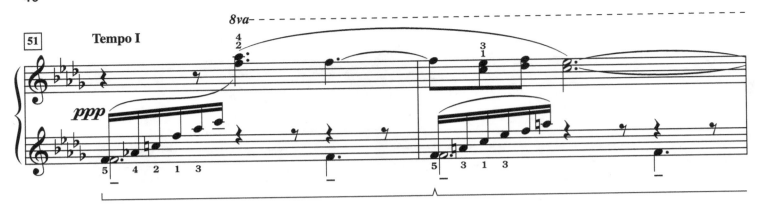

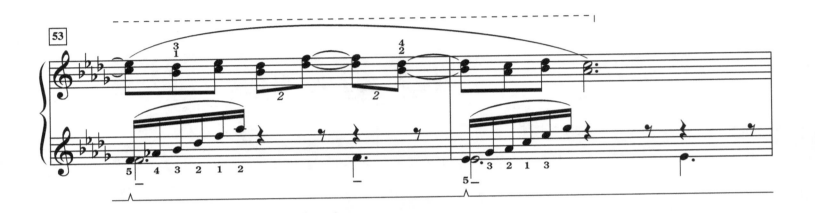

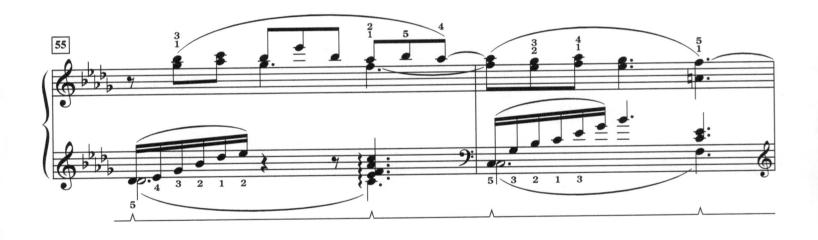

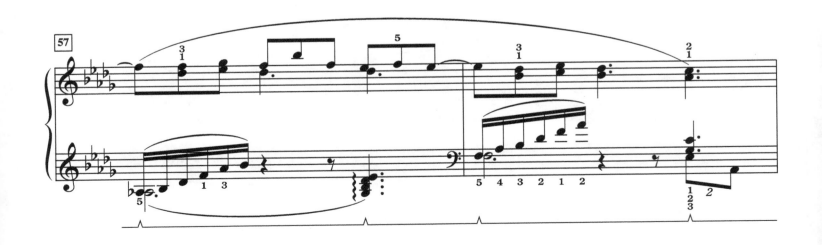

Arabesque No. 1
(from *Deux arabesques*, L. 66)

Claude Debussy
(1862–1918)

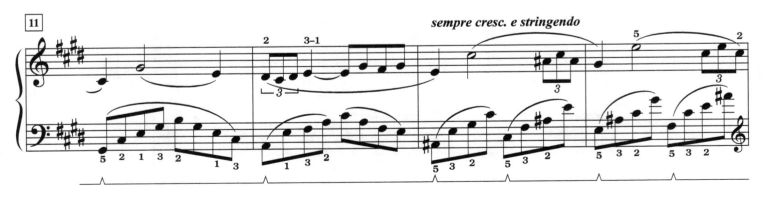

50

(a little less lively)
Tempo rubato (un peu moins vite)

La plus que lente
(*Valse pour piano*)

Claude Debussy (1862–1918)
L. 121

56

58

La fille aux cheveux de lin
(Girl with the Flaxen Hair)
(from *Préludes,* Book 1, L. 117)

Claude Debussy (1862–1918)

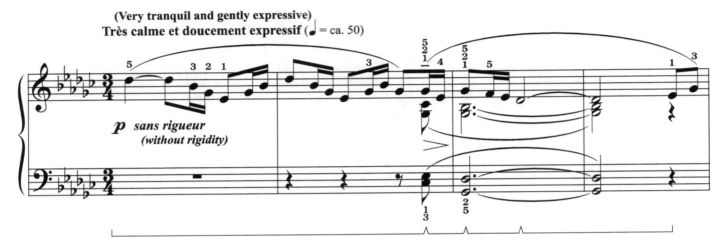

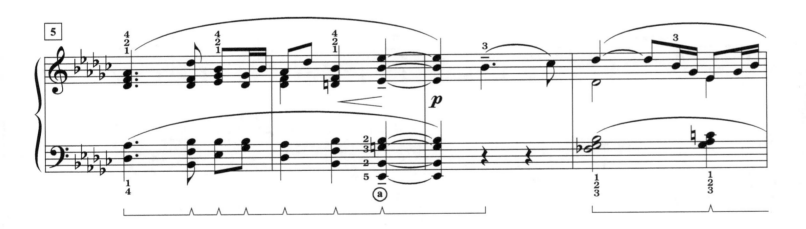

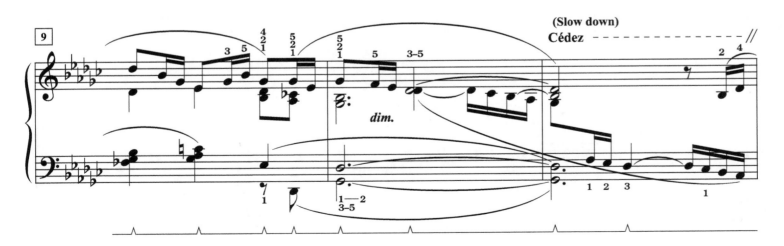

ⓐ Play the top two notes slightly after the beat, very softly.

ⓑ Play the top three notes slightly after the beat, very softly.

Prélude in D-flat Major
(from *8 pièces faciles pour piano*)

Reinhold Glière (1875–1956)
Op. 43, No. 1

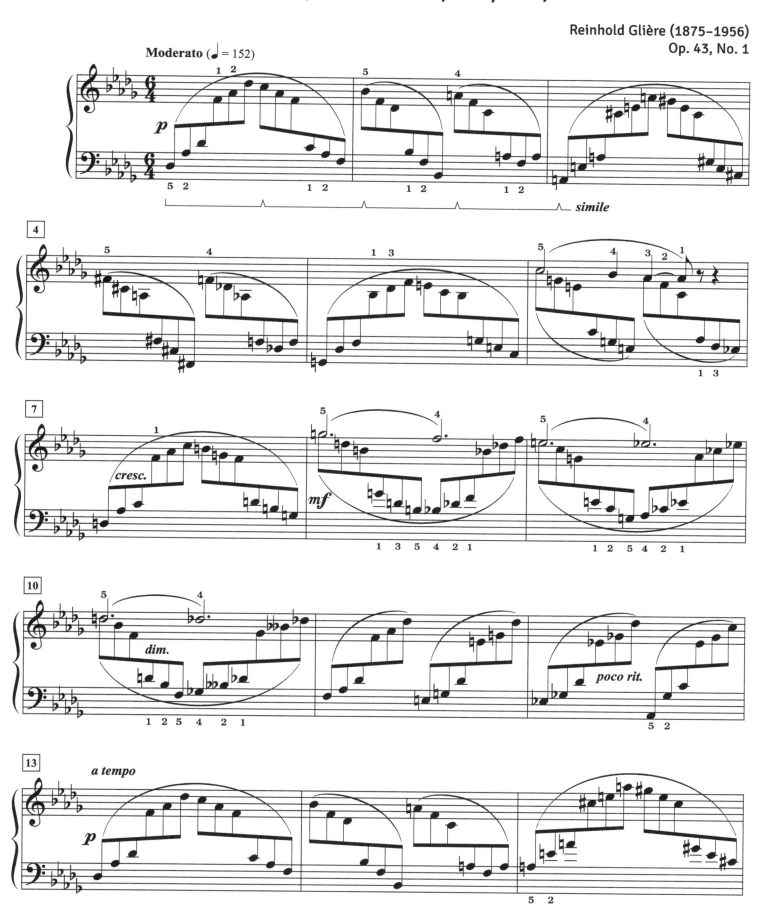

Maria
(romanza sin palabras)
(from *Six Expressive Studies*)

Enrique Granados
(1867–1916)

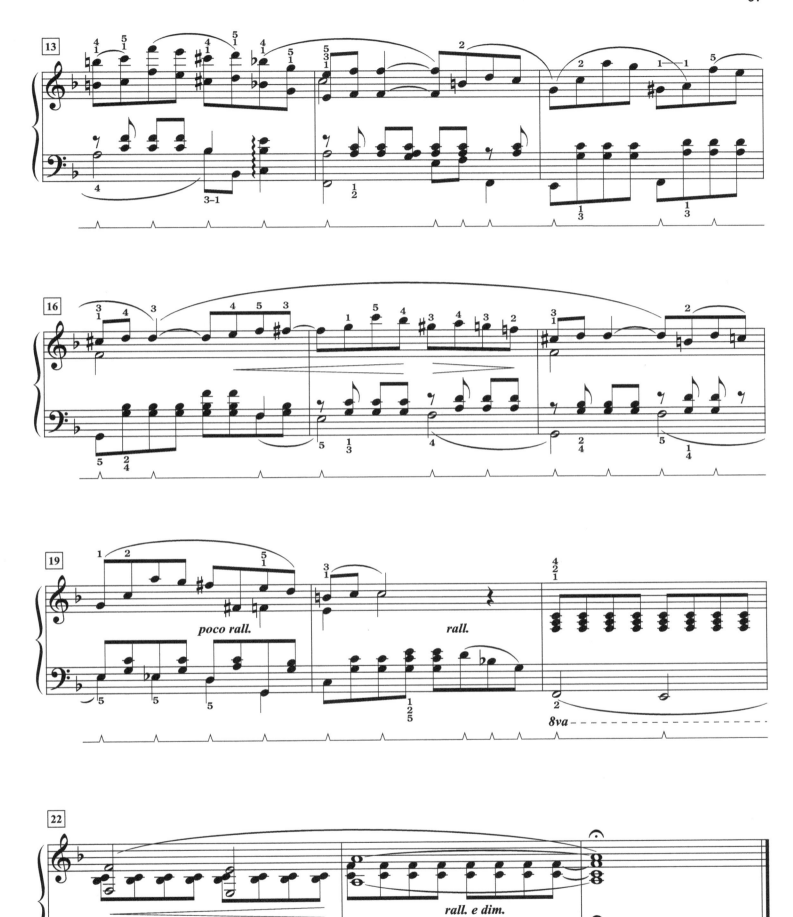

Spanish Dance No. 5
(Andaluza)
(from *12 Danzas Espagñolas*)

Enrique Granados
(1867–1916)

Andantino, quasi allegretto (♪ = 132)

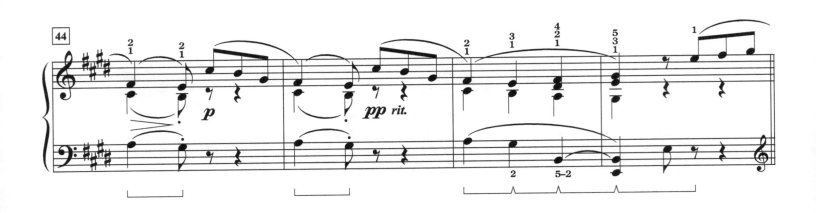

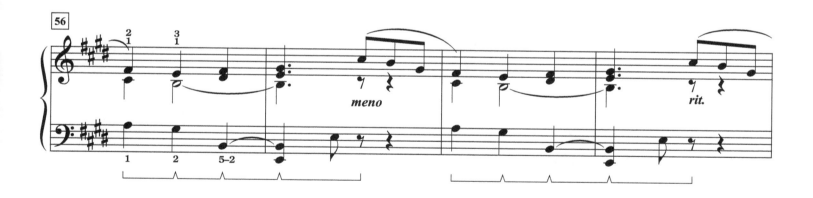

Arietta
(from *Lyric Pieces*)

Edvard Grieg (1843–1907)
Op. 12, No. 1

ⓐ Play the grace notes delicately, *before the beat.*

Notturno

(from *Lyric Pieces*)

Edvard Grieg (1843–1907)
Op. 54, No. 4

Andante (♩. = 44)

ⓐ Play the trills lightly and freely, as if each one imitates the sound of a different bird. They can begin on the main note or the upper note, at the discretion of the performer.

(Approx. Performance Time – 2:45/4:30)

The Entertainer
(A Ragtime Two Step)

Scott Joplin
(1868–1917)

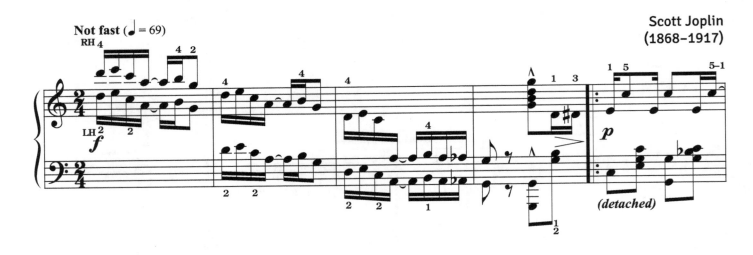

(a) To sustain the upper notes without overly blurring the accompaniment, slowly release
the pedal throughout the measure.

Maple Leaf Rag

Scott Joplin
(1868–1917)

(Approx. Performance Time – 3:45)

Ständchen ⓐ
(Serenade)

Franz Liszt (1811–1886)
S. 560, No. 7

ⓑ *Pédale à chaque Mesure*
(Pedal at each measure)

*gli accompagnamenti sempre staccato e **pp***
*(the accompaniment always staccato and **pp**)*

ⓐ Liszt transcribed this piece from the song cycle *Schwanengesang*, D. 957, by Franz Schubert (1797–1828).

ⓑ Liszt's pedaling indication.

(Approx. Performance Time – 4:45)

Consolation

Franz Liszt (1811–1886)
S. 172, No. 3

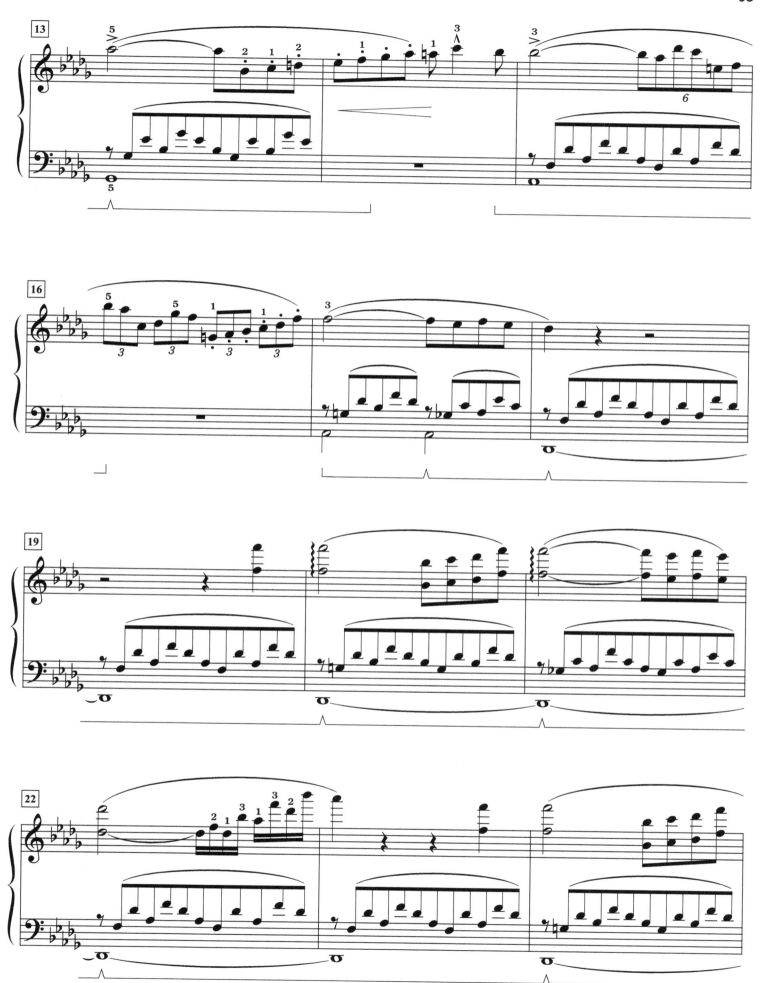

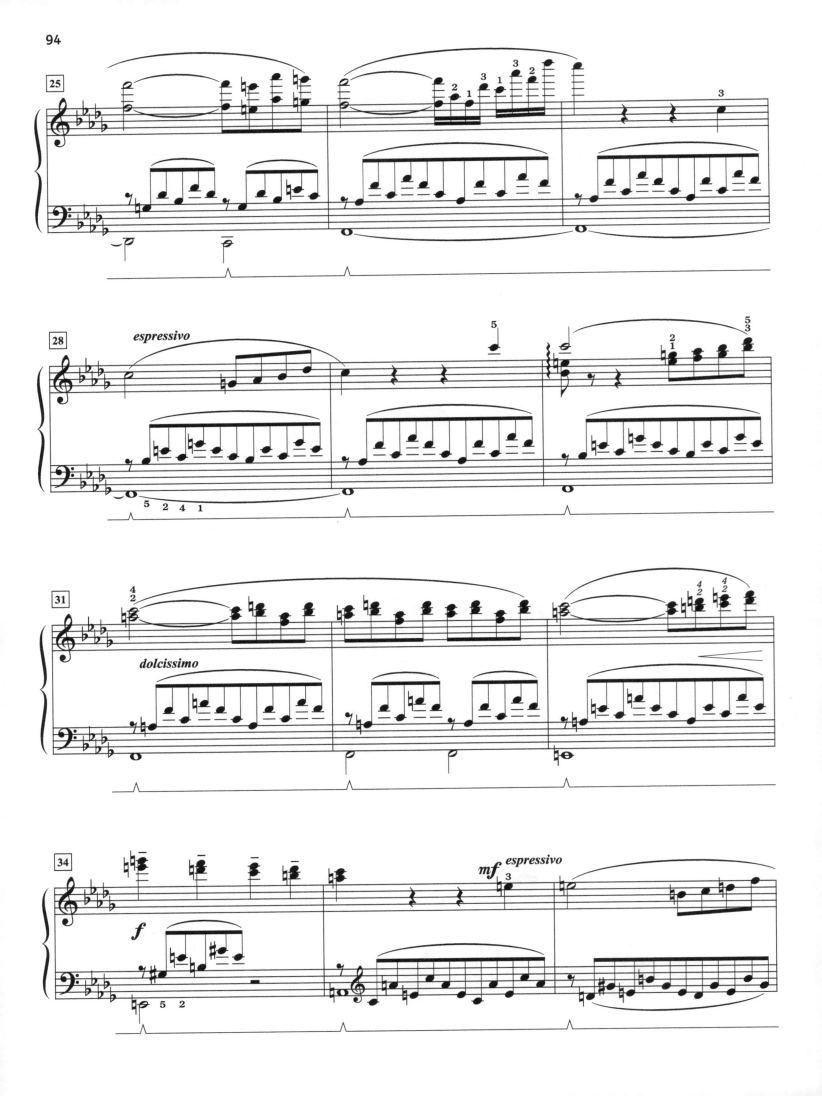

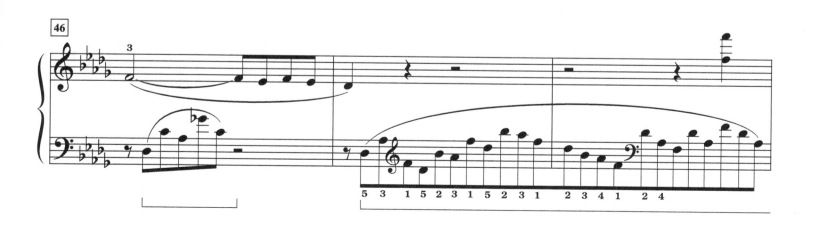

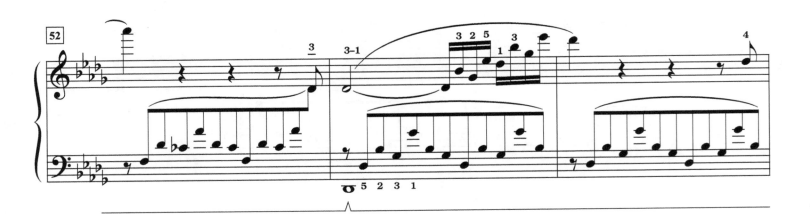

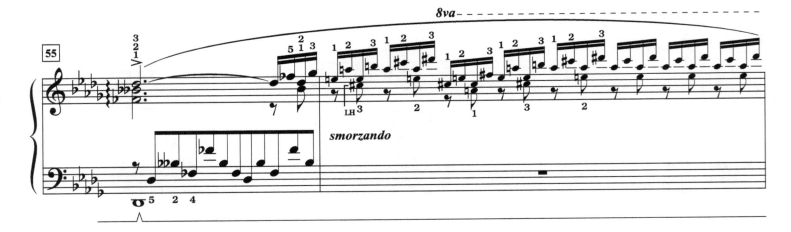

Liebeslied
(Love Song)

Franz Liszt (1811–1886)
S. 566

(a) Liszt transcribed this piece from the song cycle *Myrthen*, Op. 25, by Robert Schumann (1810–1856). The title
of the original song is "Widmung" (Dedication). Liszt arranged a few versions. This is an easier version.

To a Wild Rose
(from *Woodland Sketches*)

Edward MacDowell (1860–1908)
Op. 51, No. 1

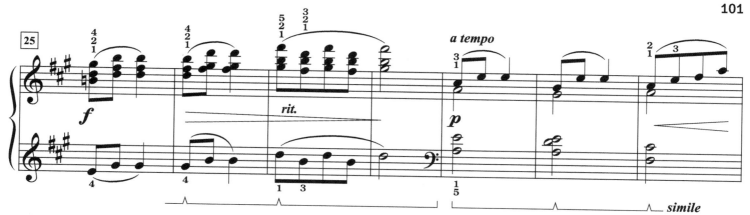

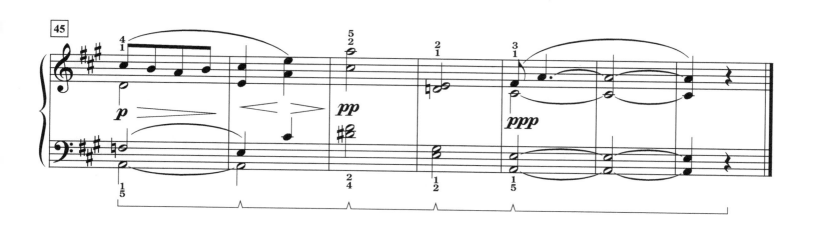

(Approx. Performance Time – 2:30/3:30)

Venetian Boat Song
(from *Songs without Words*)

Felix Mendelssohn (1809–1847)
Op. 30, No. 6

Adagio

(from *Piano Sonata in F Major*, K. 280)

Wolfgang Amadeus Mozart
(1756–1791)

ⓑ Begin the roll *on the beat.* ⓒ

(d) Play the ornaments in measures 45, 54, and 56 *on the beat*.

Andante sostenuto

(from *Songs without Words*)

Felix Mendelssohn (1809–1847)
Op. 85, No. 4

(a) Play the ornament *on the beat:*

Andante
(from *Piano Sonata in C Major*, K. 545)

Wolfgang Amadeus Mozart
(1756–1791)

Toccata
(from *Harpsichord Sonata No. 6*)

Pietro Domenico Paradisi
(1707–1791)

ⓐ The title *Toccata* is not found in the original edition, but it has been used in many editions and recordings. In the original edition of the complete sonata, this *Allegro* second movement follows a *Vivace* first movement.

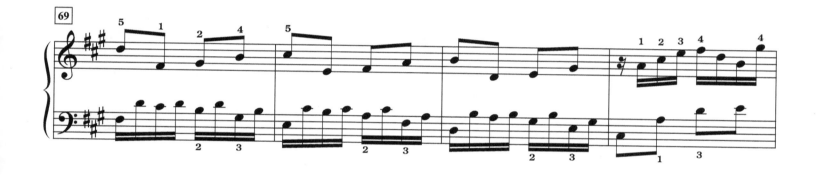

Adagio sostenuto

(from *6 moments musicaux*)

Sergei Rachmaninoff (1873–1943)
Op. 16, No. 5

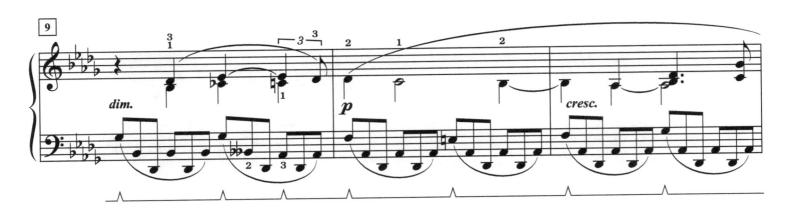

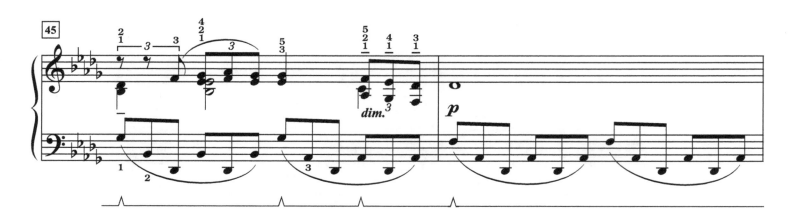

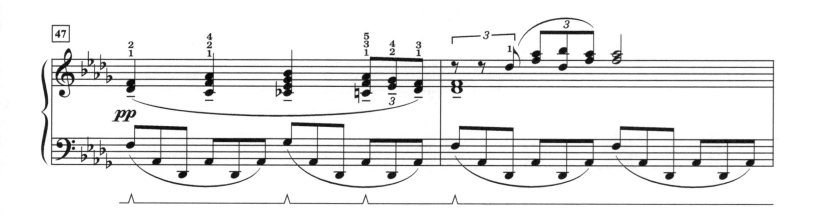

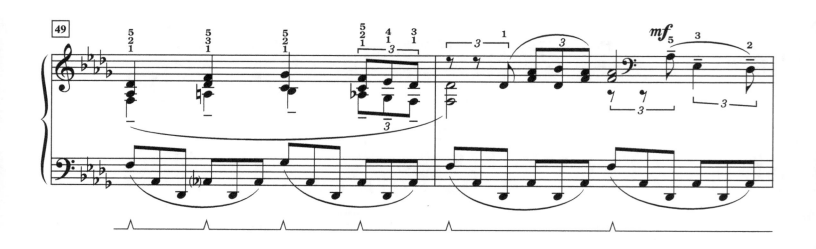

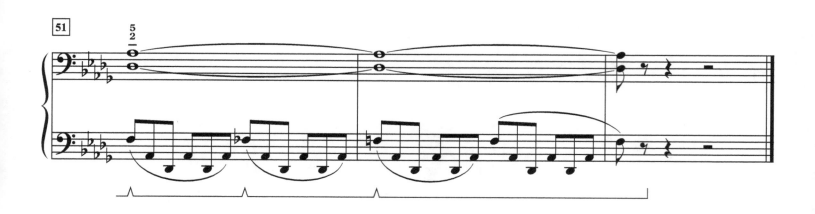

Gymnopédie No. 1

(from *Trois Gymnopédies*)

Erik Satie
(1866–1925)

(Slow and with painful sorrow)
Lent et douloureux (♩ = 76)

Mouvement de menuet

(from *Sonatine,* M. 40)

Maurice Ravel
(1825–1937)

128

Valse sentimentale
(from *34 valses sentimentales*)

Franz Schubert (1797–1828)
D. 779, No. 13

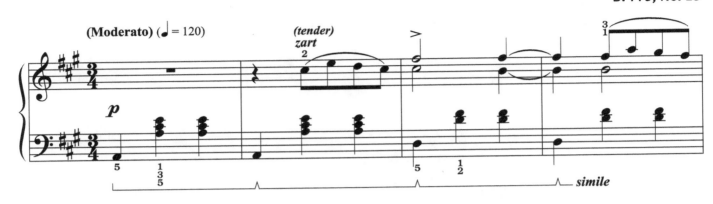

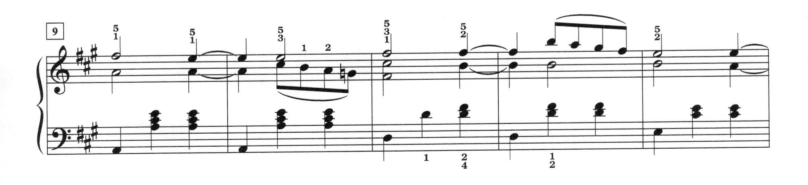

Waltz in B Minor

(from *38 Waltzes, Ländler and Ecossaises*)

Franz Schubert (1797–1828)
D. 145, No. 6

Romance in F-sharp Major
(from *3 Romanzen*)

Robert Schumann (1810–1856)
Op. 28, No. 2

ⓐ The duet between the inner voices in measures 1–8, 18–23, and 31–32 is played completely by the thumbs.

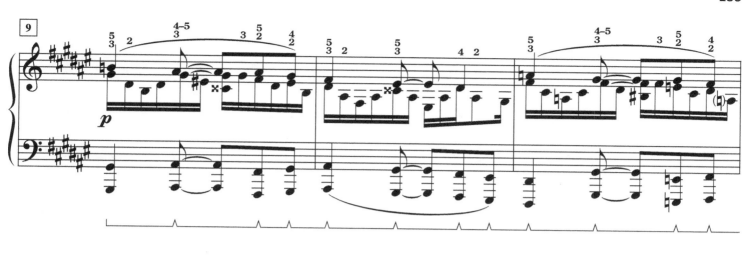

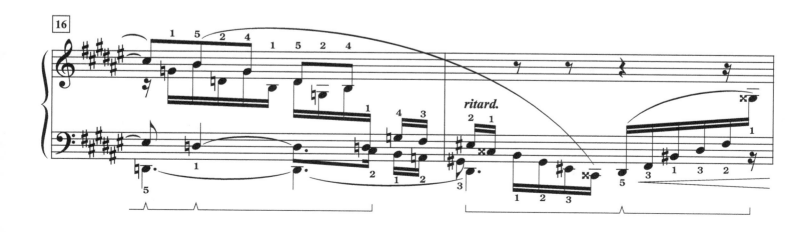

Träumerei
(from *Kinderszenen*)

Robert Schumann (1810–1856)
Op. 15, No. 7

ⓐ Play the grace notes gently, *before the beat.*

October

(from *The Seasons*)

Peter Ilyich Tchaikovsky (1840–1893)
Op. 37a, No. 10